PRISON BREAK

PRISON BREAK

Essential keys to break destructive lifestyles

ROGER CURTIS

Prison Break
Published by Roger Curtis
with Castle Publishing Ltd
New Zealand

© 2020 Roger Curtis

ISBN 978-0-473-52398-5 (Softcover)
ISBN 978-0-473-52399-2 (ePUB)
ISBN 978-0-473-52400-5 (Kindle)

Editing:
Rick Roberts & Geoff Vause

Production & Typesetting:
Andrew Killick
Castle Publishing Services
www.castlepublishing.co.nz

Cover design:
Paul Smith

All scripture quotations, unless otherwise stated,
are taken from the New King James Version®.
Copyright © 1982 by Thomas Nelson, Inc.
Used by permission. All rights reserved.

Scripture quotations marked (NLT) are taken from
The Living Bible copyright © 1971.
Used by permission of Tyndale House Publishers, Inc.,
Carol Stream, Illinois 60188.
All rights reserved.

ALL RIGHTS RESERVED

No part of this publication may be reproduced,
stored in a retrieval system, or transmitted
in any form or by any means, electronic, mechanical,
photocopying, recording or otherwise,
without prior written permission from the author.

CONTENTS

Preface	7
First Things First	9
Touch	19
The Journey Inside	23
No Ears	27
Youth	35
The One	39
Jesus Who?	43
Getting to the Start Line – Only Jesus	49
Redemption	55
Change Your Heart	61
Visit the Prisoners	67
Forgiveness	73
Deception	79
Change	83
Not Alone – Fathers	87
Steps to True Freedom	95
To Those Involved in Christian Prison Ministry	97
The Vision	99
About the Author	102

PREFACE

This book is primarily for those in prison and the Christian people ministering to them.

It is based on nearly 20 years of weekly ministry in a men's prison near Hastings in New Zealand. Some important themes are repeated throughout this book, not by accident. The apostle Peter said, 'I bring you these things by way of reminder...'

There are many testimonies, good and bad. I have employed ex-prisoners for over 30 years due to the nature of my business. Many of these men have become leading hands and foremen in the business and I have maintained contact with many others over the years. One of the men I first encountered in jail over ten years ago generously offered to proofread the manuscript.

Early on in this book, I reveal certain personal details about myself. I believe there needs to be a personal baring of the heart to truly connect with others in need. This is not 'safe' Department of Corrections policy and, in order to protect ourselves and others, such details should only be revealed with wisdom. However, this kind of heartfelt honesty is the very thing that sets Christian workers apart from secular providers entering the prisons. We are all broken people needing a saviour and our wise vulnerability allows us to truly minister the love of Christ deep into broken hearts, without condemnation.

Prison Break

As I tell all the inmates, my main reason for coming to the prison is to introduce them to Jesus so they will not come back to this place. I am trying to do myself out of a job.

FIRST THINGS FIRST

Nineteen-sixty was a good year, a vintage year. Many of my mates were born around this time. I was born in April, which makes it easy to calculate my age. We call this vintage Club 60.

They were good years. The country had pretty much recovered from World War 2 and business was good. Our family were orchardists exporting apples to Britain. These were family-owned businesses, and I remember many trips to the rail siding and to the Apple and Pear Board in town where we delivered our produce in wooden bushel cases.

Dad was my hero, while Mum kept us full of food and unconditional love. The three brothers (no sisters, yay) got up to heaps of mischief around our 40-acre orchard.

Racing tractors, go-carts, pushbikes, whatever had wheels, we made sure they broke land speed records. We enjoyed holidays all around the North Island during the summer break, until Dad decided to build a batch on the shores of Lake Taupo.

They were happy days before my teenage years arrived. I didn't realise when I was younger, but Mum and Dad were like chalk and cheese with very different upbringings. Mum was super privileged, growing up on a pastoral farm, riding horses, playing piano, attending boarding school, wanting for nothing. She was not spoilt, but her life revolved around the upper circles of society in those days.

Dad grew up on the other side of the tracks with a public education, leaving school young and starting manual work from his mid-teens.

He climbed the farming ranks to become head shepherd on a large local station. He was also a pilot, doing his training in the iconic, dual winged Tiger Moths.

They were married in the late fifties and, soon after, us boys began arriving.

Christmas was a big deal. Every year we would celebrate at Mum's family farm. The 'cuzzies' would come from all over the country and we would enjoy a week of swimming, tennis, Christmas food and presents.

Although we were welcomed and included in the activities, there was also a hint of disappointment Mum had married below her station. I eventually found out it had been a 'shotgun' wedding. I was present when my parents married.

Mum also had mental health problems and was taking medication to keep her calm. Some of the early interventions of the medical fraternity were ugly, and Dad had an extra load to carry he was not aware of when he married Mum.

When I was 12, Dad started flirting with a neighbour's wife. I pointed it out at the time, to his embarrassment. This didn't stop him and after this lady's marriage failed we saw less and less of him.

The announcement that Dad was leaving to live with her, was made while we were on one of our annual holidays at Taupo. This devastated us boys. I thought I was the worst affected and so began my life of teenage rebellion.

With only Mum at home, there was little control over me and I became abusive, disrespectful and arrogant. Dad tried at times to correct me but I quickly reminded him of his absence and rejection of us.

This had a negative effect on him and he continued to withdraw from us. What I did not know was this family disintegration was affecting my younger brothers worse than me, with my youngest brother David becoming suicidal.

As we grew up we slowly mended our relationship with Dad. We became aware of Mum's mental state and decided Dad did well to maintain the marriage as long as he did. Two of us began working with him on the orchard. We had orcharding in our blood and the three of us brothers still work in the apple industry.

My first 20 years involved a lot of interaction with working people at school and later on at the orchard. I worked alongside a lot of seasonal labourers hired for the harvest. They were rough and ready people. They came from near and far, some for long periods, others for a week or two.

There were two Māori men in particular I spent a lot of time with. One was Ron, part of a large iwi living nearby in a small settlement called Bridge Pa. He brought his family in to help. They were all good workers and were some of the first horticultural contractors in Hawkes Bay.

The second man was Windy. He was a gentle man, but boy could he work. He stayed with us well into his 70s and could still fill bins quicker than any of the younger family members he brought in to help.

I had few restraints while living at home and as I gradually gained more independence, I spent more time with my best mates, Greg and Campbell.

Motorbikes gave us freedom to go and to do, and we did. We were into fast bikes, fast cars, fast women, parties, sport, trips away.

Money in, money out. I used my Dad's V8 Chrysler during the weekends. We would 'lay rubber' and race other pretenders at night.

This all came to a screaming halt late one night when I blew the car's differential doing wheelies and had to walk to Dad's and tell him.

During the week I would borrow Mum's Austin mini. This was well before the film *Goodbye Pork Pie*. We would go where no car had ever gone before.

One night we managed to lift the car into one of the school hallways and left our calling card wheelie marks in the passage. Another night we deposited a dead cat behind the blackboard of a particularly nasty teacher.

These antics meant I would eventually run afoul of the police and traffic officers. I thought I was bulletproof. I was chased many times, mostly on my motorbike, and managed to lose them when I sped into the orchard and out the back gate.

Finally, I was caught and had to face the judge. This was one of my first big learning experiences. Although my friends all laughed at my antics, and my attempts at inclusion seemed to need updating every week, there was only one person facing the judge. I was the only one paying the penalty and my first five years driving were spent mostly as a disqualified driver.

Around this time I entered into my first serious relationship with a girl. Krystene was beautiful, clever, and, most importantly, really liked me.

We started doing life together. My mates had to take a backward step as I was hooked.

Krystene was from a broken home, living with her mother and younger sister; we even started talking about marriage. Her Mum had just started attending a small Christian fellowship, four or five families. She convinced Krystene to start attending church too.

I was not unhappy or facing any real crisis, but I had started wondering if this was all there was to life. Work, sport, drinking, party, recover, replay, it all seemed a bit aimless. Born, live, breed, die ... was there a purpose?

I had attended a traditional church with my parents when I was a child and was confirmed as an Anglican at 13. But when I was old enough to say 'no' I got out and started really living it up with my mates and our toys.

The unasked and unanswered questions stayed with me.

I did not want to lose Krystene, so I started going to some meetings. Fortifying myself with a few ales, I would duly attend and pretend to be interested.

God had other ideas. One lady I barely knew said she was praying for me. What? Praying for me? Why? I'm fine thanks, I don't need your prayers.

I began to sense a genuine love from these people. Then I started witnessing miracles. One in particular was a man who was not a Christian, had just been to hospital and had an operation to remove cancer from his stomach.

When the surgeon opened him up, he found he was riddled with terminal cancer throughout his digestive tract. They sewed him up, gave him three months to live and suggested he find a 'faith healer' because there was nothing they could do for him.

Some of the Christians prayed for him and he was healed instantly. When he returned to the hospital for a scan, they could not find any trace of the cancer. He lived many years longer.

Even Krystene was miraculously healed from something called a 'lazy eye'. She had already had an operation to correct one of her eyes and was booked in to have the other done. After prayer she was examined again and found she did not need the operation.

Other miraculous things happened. I saw ordinary people simply believing the Bible was current and true, and God was backing them up when they prayed.

I also began to think if there was indeed a 'god' then maybe there was a purpose to life and a hope for the future after all.

I was conflicted for a while because I enjoyed what I saw as 'freedom', and there was also a number of things disturbing me based on my own life experience. If I wanted things to be better in the future, I knew my good intentions were not going to be enough.

Krystene decided she was to continue her education in Auckland and I was all for this. We could still maintain a long-distance relationship. I was also hearing another voice saying, 'Don't do anything further about this God stuff, she will be gone soon and you will be able to get back to normal with all your mates.'

That Sunday was just another day, but I knew what I had to do. Without being asked or compelled by anyone, I asked to speak to the church leader who was coincidentally a police sergeant. He and two other men led me in what is called a salvation prayer. I knew nothing about spiritual things and was ignorant concerning most of the Bible except the Christmas story and a little about Easter.

What happened next overwhelmed me.

I was sitting on a stool when I prayed and what I can only describe as an invisible torrent of something pure started washing through me from my head to my toes. This power hit me and flipped me off the stool and laid me on the floor. I remember the power and the tears, lots of tears. It felt like all the ugly, damaging, corrupt filth and grime infecting my soul was being washed out of me. That was the tears.

I thought it was only for a minute and I was told later I was on the floor for 15 minutes speaking in tongues, as described in Acts 2:

First Things First

> On the day of Pentecost all the believers were meeting together in one place. Suddenly, there was a sound from heaven like the roaring of a mighty windstorm, and it filled the house where they were sitting. Then, what looked like flames or tongues of fire appeared and settled on each of them. And everyone present was filled with the Holy Spirit and began speaking in other languages as the Holy Spirit gave them this ability. (Acts 2:1-4, NLT)

Obviously, this was a life-changing moment. It doesn't happen to everyone who turns to God. In the Bible we are told to operate by faith, not by feelings. I am relaying to you my experience. Little did I know my new commitment was going to be severely tested over the next three months.

After six weeks Krystene came back from Auckland and announced our relationship was over, she was moving on. I was devastated as we had been talking about marriage. We were both now Christians. Surely things were only going to get better.

She was resolute, and I had a decision to make. Was I going to run to God or away from God? These new Christian friends of mine were nothing like me. I still liked fast cars, travelling, hanging with the men. These Christians were the sort of people I stayed away from at school. They were a little weird, a bit too clean, do-gooders, teachers liked them.

I could not doubt God's renewing power surging through me. I was already changing, while many of my worldly mates had started rejecting me, saying I had found 'religion'. I was busy trying to convince them there really was a God, he loved them and wanted them to join the family of God.

They didn't get it, and I was left alone.

I chose God. I realised any other path was a downhill decision. I was no longer searching for the truth. I had found the truth.

Over the next two years I continued to attend church at Flaxmere. This suburb of Hastings has a dark reputation from gang affiliation, struggling families, violence and unemployment. I was the only 'weirdo' in my family, according to my Dad, and as long as that was the case he could handle it. But I was working on my brothers, inviting them to some Christian outings and generally challenging them about their futile lives

They gave me the staunch reply, laughed in my face and belittled my new lifestyle.

But myself and others were praying for them, and about two years after I had turned to Jesus they both did the same thing within 24 hours of each other. Little did I know at the time, but David, my youngest brother, had been about to commit suicide. He had the gun and ammunition ready in his bedroom, but that day changed everything for him.

Those were great days. Instead of being the minority, we were now the majority in our family. Dad lost the plot. He had a negative experience with religion when he was younger and was furious his three boys had joined a 'cult'.

We had many arguments, some almost coming to physical violence, but he was pretty clear we had to make a decision, either the orchard and our inheritance, or the church; it could not be both.

We chose Jesus. He kicked us off the orchard and denied us our inheritance. He kept his word and, when he died, all the money went to his second wife. We did not contest this, but I truly believe we made the right decision. Something Jesus said confirmed our decision:

> So Jesus answered and said, 'Assuredly, I say to you, there is no one who has left house or brothers or sisters or father or mother or wife or children or lands, for my sake and the

gospel's, who shall not receive a hundredfold now in this time – houses and brothers and sisters and mothers and children and lands, with persecutions – and in the age to come, eternal life.' (Mark 10:29-30)

Dad was so angry he wanted us off the property in the middle of the harvest. We persuaded him to allow us to stay and finish, he consented, but as soon as the last apple was picked we were gone. Was I angry? No, just sad. Many fathers want their children to continue in the same occupation as themselves and many times this simply doesn't happen. In this case, Dad had three boys keen to continue his legacy and because of his feelings about our choice of Christianity, he lost us.

We left home with no more than a suitcase each. I started boarding with one of my Christian mates and my brothers ended up in a caravan in his back yard. Flaxmere was our new home.

We all started working on different orchards. Not long after, my brother Philip and I started an orchard contracting business and have been going ever since. We are now the longest-serving pip fruit contractors in Hawkes Bay

Our passion for the apple industry has increased over the years, and one of my brothers has the email address 'borntoprune'. We also have another enduring passion, to reach the lost for Christ. Some of the people we were now employing lived in Flaxmere, their lives in constant turmoil, and we knew we had the answer.

We had to do something.

TOUCH

Ron Georgie Park 2 pm Sunday afternoon. Be there.

A young couple in the fellowship lived across the road from this non-descript park in the south-west corner of Flaxmere. There were a few of us playing sport for local clubs on Saturday. On Sunday we met at the park to enjoy two hours of touch rugby.

This was before touch competitions existed. We made our own rules, and because most of the men were keen on rugby league we stuck to league rules. On the last touch you were allowed to kick the ball as long as it travelled over ten metres.

It started with about six people. Slowly the word began to spread in the street there was a touch game to be had every Sunday afternoon, run by some crazy Christians. We supplied the ref and used the bright red road cones as corner markers. When more people turned up we moved the cones further out.

More people began to come and, at the height, over 70 people would show up. With about 35 players on each side, we split the game into two fields, but the men all wanted to play in the same game so the field ended up being twice the size of a normal rugby field.

We had gangsters, we had street kids, Rastafarians – we didn't care, the game was the bait to attract everybody. We supplied drink and food at half time to get them in close to hear.

We preached the gospel winter summer, autumn, spring. It didn't matter, we were always there, rain, hail, sun, or wind, we always turned up.

Drug dealers turned up to do their business, police would quietly cruise past knowing what was going down, but the men were quiet and respectful to the Word. They listened, some had questions, but mostly they were there for the game. We didn't have a PA system, so I had to position myself upwind so they could all hear.

We tried different sports during the summer, but the numbers dropped, so we went back to Touch – 12 months a year for 13 years, every Sunday. We learnt a lot of lessons through those years. It was challenging speaking to the same audience every week. The message had to be fresh, relevant and interesting, otherwise they would walk away.

I had to learn the language of the street. Trying to explain Christian principles was always a challenge. I would like to say we had great success, but over the years we saw only a handful of people turn to the Lord. They are still part of our church, some now in leadership roles. If the Lord had told me I was going to preach for over 13 years for little or no result, I don't know if I would have even started.

Years later we had people say they are now Christians and what happened out on the park was a stepping stone to their conversion. It's sowing seed – you have to sow before you can harvest.

I was often the referee, and one day one of the men got so angry with my decision he came over and punched me in the face. The other men rushed in and hauled him away. He left in disgrace; he had crossed a line.

Later that day he turned up at my home to apologise. He got saved that day. I heard on another day after the game three men were talking at the local shop. One of them was belittling what I had said, and another one hit him and told him to shut up. He came back three weeks later with a lot more respect.

Sometimes there would be distractions. Local clubs started running a league competition on the same park. We got squeezed into a small corner and at half time most of the men left to watch the other games.

One day I was annoyed and refused to bring the Word, until I saw one guy waiting and looking around, obviously waiting for the Word. He looked slightly embarrassed because nothing was happening.

This was a huge lesson to me. Even if there was only one person listening, I needed to bring the Word. It's not about numbers.

The greatest thing those years taught us was to be resilient and persistent. One year we decided to put together a Christian team to compete in the local touch competition. We would constantly lose and were looked upon as easy beats, but we continued to train and slowly improved.

In the last tournament of the year we started winning a few games and made it to the final. The team we were playing had never been beaten. They were stacked with rep players and were super confident. We beat them.

There was much embarrassment at the presentation as the other team's name had already been engraved on the cup. The organisers apologised and we received the cup two days later. It pays to persevere.

After 13 years and much prayer, we decided it was time to finish. We made the announcement one Sunday. There was genuine disappointment from the men and some vowed to continue without us. Some turned up for the next few weeks, but the numbers dropped and soon it finished altogether. We

Prison Break

Christians were the glue keeping this going for so long. There must be a sermon in there somewhere.

It was to be a few years before another effective door for ministry would open.

THE JOURNEY INSIDE

In 2000 I started ministering at the local prison with two of my close friends.

We were initially invited as backup, playing a few songs and bringing the love of Christ into the inmates' lives. What amazed me was the number of familiar faces from the 'outside'. This was a second home to many of them.

One of my seasonal employees was there, locked up for drunk driving. He was shocked to see me. It seemed he could not get away from these crazy Christians wherever he went. I followed his journey through the prison system until he was released, and returned to work with me.

I had another two Christian brothers in the business at the time and between us, we worked on him. It took two more years and eventually he surrendered his life to Jesus.

This guy had been in and out of prison all his adult life, had strong connections with the biggest gang in town, a broken marriage, lost kids, deep in debt, a violent man.

I have had the privilege of walking with this guy for many years now. He is out of debt, which was around $40,000, reunited with his children, is involved with night security around our town and has faithfully attended church all that time. His life has truly and radically changed.

Many men in prison want an instant solution to all their

problems. They pray to get released early and it never happens, things are going very wrong with their family outside the wire and they can do little about it. They want to know where God is.

I explain it usually isn't one big bad decision putting them in prison, it's lots of little *bad* decisions. God isn't so interested in their early release as much as fixing their broken hearts. Real change begins by making lots of *good* little decisions.

Picture this: A man has dug a deep hole and is now trapped at the bottom, unable to climb out. He shouts out to Jesus, expecting him to lean down and lift him out of the hole. Instead, Jesus shows up and throws a decent shovel down the hole and jumps in with his own shovel to help fill the hole in. When they've finished, the man is standing at ground level and can't fall back down the hole because it's no longer there. If Jesus had simply lifted him out, there would still be a hole to fall into again.

I have found over the years the journey from prison is not short or simple. It takes time, sweat, good decisions, guts to swim against the tide. It also needs someone who will walk alongside to encourage, direct, correct, and urge on to the finish line. Over the years I have seen many men turn to Jesus while locked up, only to quickly forget and give up when they return to 'normal' life. There needs to be a bridge between jail and the outside world.

I have employed many of these men and they have become team leaders in my company. All they needed was someone who believed they could change. They in turn have reached out and helped others as they try to 'get straight'.

I have also been astounded by the number of workmates and family who continue to ridicule these men. Government institutions also continue to remind them about their past. Employers refuse to take them on, even years after they have completed their sentences. No wonder many give up and become resigned to the fact they are never going to reform, and decide to hang out with the people who helped get them into trouble in the first place.

The reoffending rates tell a sad story. One third are reconvicted within 12 months of release, 50 percent after three years. There are many programmes run in the prison to help rehabilitate these men. These programmes are better than nothing, but they do little to lower reoffending rates. Successive governments frequently abandon efforts to reduce the appalling recidivist rates.

It's not enough to get somebody to change their mind because this can be very short-term. People change their mind on a daily basis.

For meaningful change you need to speak to the heart. Out of the heart flow the issues of life.

> Keep your heart with all diligence, for out of it spring the issues of life. (Proverbs 4:23)

> Guard your heart above all else, for it determines the course of your life. (NLT)

NO EARS

People may listen, but they don't always hear.

Most of the groups I've spoken to in prison attended voluntarily. This is important because they're willing to hear something fresh, something new, or maybe a different perspective.

You can't progress with anyone if they refuse to listen. This is often known as the 'victim mentality'. It's always someone else's fault – family, mates, police, or even the government.

One of the hardest sessions I had was with some men who had been complaining for weeks they always missed out on church. The other wings always got preferential treatment and they were left out.

One Sunday it was decided to let them go to church first. What a disaster. They came in and immediately started complaining about how hard-done-by they were, blaming the officers, staff, and even other inmates in other wings for their situation.

They became agitated and one became quite violent. We couldn't reason with them, so we sat quietly and let them vent. The whole session was all about them. We accomplished zero. If people are not ready to hear, it's better to move on.

Stewart was now in his late 40s on his fourth lag and was just starting to realise he needed to get off this life-wasting circuit. He had a struggling wife and three young children. She remained faithful to him, but this time he was thinking it was time for a change.

Over the years he had done all the courses on offer, so this time he decided to come and hear what the Christians had to say. He came to ten two-hour sessions.

Stewart became a changed man. Half way through the course he confessed that over the last 30 years, he was not interested in anything Christians had to say and preaching at him would have done nothing to change his destructive behaviour. He had not been ready to hear.

Using the tool of prayer is important for those bringing the gospel into the prisons. Only God can soften the hardest heart and move people to a point of receiving his life-changing Word.

Another reason people are deaf to the gospel is because they have no idea there is a God, or Jesus or Holy Spirit. In Jesus's day there was already a basic societal understanding there is a God in heaven. This belief was passed down from generation to generation.

This was also the case in this country until recently. Now, sadly, it is not uncommon for two or three generations to have no knowledge of the Living God and the story of salvation. Many times I have had to start from the position of convincing people there is in fact a God who loves and cares for them.

Some are deaf because they believe in many gods and 'why should I believe in only one God?' I usually respond with a question. Have any of your prayers been answered by any of these gods, have they even heard your prayers?

Some have asked if they can continue belonging to a gang and be a Christian. This is untenable for a number of reasons:

> Do not be deceived: 'Evil company corrupts good habits.' (1 Corinthians 15:33)

Who you are hanging with usually determines which direction you go in life. Some have said they want to reach out to other gang members and turn them to Jesus. This is commendable, and usually a heartfelt desire, but the pressure of gang association usually influences you more than you influencing them.

Many use prison as a type of detox. Coming off drugs 'cold turkey' is difficult, but most appreciate the break from addiction. Released back into gang culture means drugs are freely available and inevitably leads back to the habit and bondage.

Many gang associates have families who suffer greatly while the man is locked up. The gang promises to look after them while dad is inside. This is not a charitable offer, it's a 'tick up' and in order to repay the debt, the men are forced back into gang culture when they are released.

Lisa is a gang associate. Her man was the 'Prez' of a local chapter. She had been beaten many times and often turned up on our doorstep needing hospital treatment. She was reliant on him for her drug habit and had two little girls to him. The drugs were killing her. She ended up in Wellington hospital facing an operation with only a ten percent survival rate. She called us and we prayed the salvation prayer together and prayed the operation would be successful.

Ten days later she returned home and came to stay with us. Two weeks before the operation she had broken up with him and was now trying to begin a new life outside the gang.

A week later I was in the prison taking a Sunday service in the same unit where her man was. Ten men attended, the subject we discussed was suicide. I left before lunch and 30 minutes later they found him dead in his cell by suicide.

This devastated many of his gang associates. This was a Prez and these men are supposed to be at the top of the feeding chain. Many of them aspired to be like him, yet here he was, dead.

His death reverberated around the prison for over a year with many of them asking me for my perspective on why, because they had no answers. Some would ask the question and give their reasons without listening for a reply. No ears.

The tangi a week later was attended by gang chapters from around the North Island. This guy was honoured more in death than life. I don't know why he killed himself. I do know he had access to drugs and was living with a high level of paranoia. He was also offered counsel and help from Christians which he refused to hear.

Lisa was devastated and blamed herself for his death. She was also told it was her fault by other gang members.

Then began the slow and gentle process to heal both mind and body. While she stayed with us, improvement was steady. She started attending church, looking after her girls and physically became stronger, lowering her dependence on medication.

Lisa wanted to reach into the gang and lead them to Christ. Our advice was it was far too soon. She was not strong enough and would probably be influenced by them.

Then it started. Over a three to four month period, six gang members killed themselves. Whether or not this was some perverse reaction to the Prez, these men thought they would go out with a bang. Lisa attended all these tangi and was immersed in gang culture again. She started using again and soon moved out from the sanctuary of our home.

She was recently readmitted to hospital for the same problems she had before. We fear for her life and pray once again, in his mercy, God will intervene and deliver her and her children from this futile, destructive life.

The Bible speaks plainly about these matters:

> But it has happened to them according to the true proverb: 'A dog returns to his own vomit,' and, 'a sow, having washed, to her wallowing in the mire.' (2 Peter 2:22)

I don't pretend to know all the psychological reasons for these events, but I do know who was behind them.

His name is Satan, the deceiver. Many people are ignorant of his existence or are under the impression he is their friend, and hell is not so bad. Both perceptions are wrong and reinforce their being deceived by one who is the greatest deceiver.

He deceived one-third of the angels in heaven he was worth following more than God himself. He deceived Man in the Garden of Eden it was possible to disobey God without negative consequences and it would improve their lot. The devil or Satan may entice with drugs and illicit sex, but his plan is to kill as quickly as possible. He has always been a murderer.

> You are of your father the devil, and the desires of your father you want to do. He was a murderer from the beginning, and does not stand in the truth, because there is no truth in him. When he speaks a lie, he speaks from his own resources, for he is a liar and the father of it. (John 8:44)

Jesus, who does not lie, describes him as a thief. To those who do not believe in a devil, I ask: Has there been any stealing, killing or destroying in your life? If there has, then Satan has been at work in your life. You may not be able to see him, but you can feel his effects

> The thief does not come except to steal, and to kill, and to destroy. I have come that they may have life, and that they may have it more abundantly. (John 10:10)

Until you register there is a God and there is a devil, you will be stumbling around in the dark and your ears will be closed to the Good News.

> But he who hates his brother is in darkness and walks in darkness, and does not know where he is going, because the darkness has blinded his eyes. (1 John 2:11)

Being closed to the gospel is described in the parable of the sower Jesus told in Matthew 13:

> Then he spoke many things to them in parables, saying: 'Behold, a sower went out to sow. And as he sowed, some seed fell by the wayside; and the birds came and devoured them... 'Therefore hear the parable of the sower: When anyone hears the word of the kingdom, and does not understand it, then the wicked one comes and snatches away what was sown in his heart. This is he who received seed by the wayside. (Matthew 13:3-4, 18-19)

The wayside is hard ground or the pathway beside the cultivated field. This is a hard heart, and the seed (word of God) sits on the surface, then the birds (Satan) come and immediately snatch the seed

There are times when we need to persevere in sowing the word of God. There is nothing wrong with the seed. It is the condition of the recipient's heart determining how effective this will be. This hard or fallow ground needs to be broken up in order for the word of God to penetrate.

In any group you are going to find different hearts, and sometimes a direct or challenging word needs to be spoken. This can lead to change. No one likes change, yet it is one of the only constants in our lives. Challenge produces pressure, pressure produces change; no challenge, no pressure; no pressure, no change.

YOUTH

There is a youth wing in the local prison I have been ministering at for many years. The upper age limit is 19 years, and young men come from all over the North Island.

In many cases these are second and third generation criminals. They have grown up knowing only abuse and broken families. They are attracted to the gang scene where they are accepted, not judged, and find a certain level of security amongst their peers. Prison is often a rite of passage, and part of their mana, or pecking order, is established by spending time inside.

The local prison is low to medium security and the youth unit tends to be one of the more volatile units. There have been many Sundays we could not get in because there had been an incident. Testosterone levels are high and many strut around like peacocks. It's not until they are moved to the adult wings they get a dose of reality and realise just how far down the pecking order they are.

Some have come from good stable homes with loving parents but have chosen to go the way of the rebel and have ended up here. Some are contrite but don't say much for fear of being labelled weak or soft.

Acceptance by their peers is right up there on their list of importance, so many wear a mask to hide what is really happening inside them.

To have a life-changing impact you need to establish a relationship with them. At one stage I had access on a fortnightly basis over a three-month period to a core group of four young men who meant business with God. They were not afraid to carry their Bibles around and were keen to attend any spiritual programmes on offer.

They were having a positive influence on the others and on one Sunday, 12 of them showed up for the church service. Genuine questions were asked and answered. We preached the gospel and at the end of the session they all prayed the salvation prayer. They prayed loud and proud, they were not ashamed; there were high fives and genuine joy. They did not want us to go; they were like sponges soaking up the word and presence of God.

Some of these guys we would not see again, so we had to trust God to take care of them. They may forget the prayer but God won't. For others this was a life-changing moment; their journey with Jesus had just started.

I find those who have had an encounter with God remember it well – a divine moment, an answer to prayer, the presence of God in their cell. They keep these events close to their heart and only reveal these moments to people they trust.

We need to become those people. I told them to mark this day, remember it forever, for this was the day they were 'Born Again'.

> Jesus answered, 'Most assuredly, I say to you, unless one is born of water and the Spirit, he cannot enter the kingdom of God. That which is born of the flesh is flesh, and that which is born of the Spirit is spirit. Do not marvel that I said to you, 'You must be born again.' (John 3:5-7)

My heart goes out to these young men because they still have most of their lives to live. The decisions they make will have a huge bearing on their life and, most importantly, will negatively or positively affect those around them.

We have many of these intersections in our life where we can change our destination.

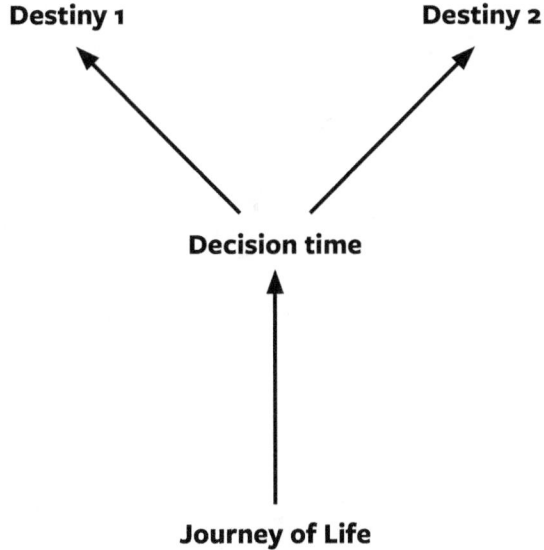

When you are young, these little or big decisions place you on a certain path, either life or death. There are always consequences. The younger you are, the greater distance you have to walk down whatever path you have chosen, so your destination ends up miles away from where you started.

Salvation is so important as it steers them on a new path, a righteous path, and begins a most exciting journey through life.

THE ONE

I gradually began to judge my effectiveness in the prison by the number of men who would attend each session.

Less than five was considered a failure. As I developed strong relationships with them, I found it harder to abandon them when the numbers dropped. Jesus reminded me he left the 99 to search for the one.

> If a man has a hundred sheep and one of them wanders away, what will he do? Won't he leave the ninety-nine others on the hills and go out to search for the one that is lost? (Matthew 18:12, NLT)

He also reminded me about Phillip in Acts 8 who started a revival in Samaria and was called by an angel of God to leave it and go into the desert to minister to a single Ethiopian eunuch.

Unlike the mandatory programmes run by Corrections, ours were voluntary. We were getting those who wanted to be there. As they were challenged to live a new life, some dropped out, but the stayers were absorbing and growing, longing to become better men, primarily for themselves, but also for their families.

God introduced me to one man who illustrates the value he ascribes to the individual.

Ted was a 'double lifer', always at odds with the wardens. He was a very angry man. Ted grew up in a big city in a loving family. His early years were uneventful until his parents split, sending him into a downward spiral of drugs, violence and illicit relationships. There was one person he stayed close to, his younger sister. He was her protector, her guide, and he loved her deeply

She was brutally raped and killed by two men. Ted killed them in revenge and what he thought was justice. He was given a double life sentence and spent time in the high security Paremoremo prison.

Through the years he was moved around to many different prisons. I first met him in a bed unit in Mangaroa. Ted was passionate about his Bible. He first came to know about Jesus in Paremoremo in a life-changing moment. He carried a worn-out Bible which had obviously been studied a lot.

He immediately challenged my authority in coming into the prison. He liked to dominate and intimidate. He held the floor for long periods, and I could see he was annoying the other men. We had some frank exchanges.

This cleared the air and we soon grew to respect one another. As the numbers attending the lessons began to drop, he and I ended up one on one. This lasted for about three months on a weekly basis. I looked forward to these encounters as he slowly began to open up and share his deepest thoughts, fears, hopes and struggles.

This was not a one-way conversation as I too shared some of my journey with him. He had a reputation of being a difficult, abusive, manipulating person. He had few real friends, the officers hated dealing with him and he was moved around a lot. This greatly frustrated him because he knew he should not be this way.

Romans 7 describes this dilemma:

And I know that nothing good lives in me, that is, in my sinful nature I want to do what is right, but I can't. I want to do what is good, but I don't. I don't want to do what is wrong, but I do it anyway. But if I do what I don't want to do, I am not really the one doing wrong; it is sin living in me that does it.

I have discovered this principle of life – that when I want to do what is right, I inevitably do what is wrong. I love God's law with all my heart. But there is another power within me that is at war with my mind. This power makes me a slave to the sin that is still within me. Oh, what a miserable person I am! Who will free me from this life that is dominated by sin and death? (Romans 7:18-24, NLT)

As I began to pray for him, the Lord showed me he had not truly repented. Repentance is how we enter into the presence of God. It takes a change of mind and heart to stop going our own way and humbly apologise to God realising the need to truly change and to start walking toward God, instead of away.

Ted was moved to tears when I shared a story about one of my sons, who, in his mid-teens, had been getting up to mischief without us parents knowing. One day as he was mowing the lawn, God spoke to him about confessing and putting it right. He parked the mower in the middle of the lawn and promptly biked around to my pastor and confessed all to him. Then he came home and told us.

I think this story moved Ted because my son did this himself with no other human intervention. Ted had heard the same voice but had been unable to respond properly, and he carried this anger and resentment inside him for many years.

We spent three months talking about repentance. There were many tears and at the end of it all, Ted had truly changed. He tried to put things right with the wardens but they would have none of it. They had seen this too many times so were unable to forgive and move on.

Ted was eventually moved to another prison and continues to communicate with me. He wrote to me:

> I truly enjoyed our one-on-one time together, being in your company and having everything in common. I've never forgotten those times of true worship in Spirit and truth, my love for Jesus will never diminish.

Recently Ted got to share the word of God with a dying inmate, sitting with him and being a servant to him. The man died peacefully. I don't know if Ted will ever be released, but I do know he has found peace with God and peace with himself, something many seek but few obtain.

JESUS WHO?

We are living in challenging times in New Zealand.

A nation long experiencing the gentle redeeming touch of the Lord over many generations has largely become a secular unbelieving society with no moral anchor. God has been relegated to the history basket and many young people have no idea there even is a God.

> You should know this, Timothy that in the last days there will be very difficult times. For people will love only themselves and their money. They will be boastful and proud, scoffing at God, disobedient to their parents, and ungrateful. They will consider nothing sacred. They will be unloving and unforgiving; they will slander others and have no self-control. They will be cruel and hate what is good. They will betray their friends, be reckless, be puffed up with pride, and love pleasure rather than God. They will act religious, but they will reject the power that could make them godly. Stay away from people like that. (2 Timothy 3:1-5, NLT)

This lack of knowledge about God and Jesus has now become inter-generational. Being asked to 'prove God exists' is not uncommon. Explaining God in some religious or theological context convinces nobody. The best way to bring about an awareness of God is by personal testimony, life-changing testimony. I once was lost but now am found.

No one can disprove your personal testimony. It happened, it was powerful, confronting, cleansing, and spiritual. I prayed ... God showed up and answered my prayer.

Moving people to acceptance of God and salvation is due to the power of the Holy Spirit. It is a gift. It is the grace of God. Somebody needs to prayerfully intercede on behalf of these lost souls; it should be you. Jesus walked in Israel 2000 years ago. This is an historical fact, but how that relates to us today is by way of the cross. Jesus died once for all.

> Under the old covenant, the priest stands and ministers before the altar day after day, offering the same sacrifices again and again, which can never take away sins. But our High Priest offered himself to God as a single sacrifice for sins, good for all time. Then he sat down in the place of honour at God's right hand. There he waits until his enemies are humbled and made a footstool under his feet. For by that one offering he forever made perfect those who are being made holy. (Hebrews 10:11-14, NLT)

Seeing is not believing. First believe, then you will *see*. Jesus said:

> Blessed are those who believe without seeing me. (John 20:29, NLT)

The Israelites saw and experienced God for 40 years. First the fire, smoke and earthquake; when God descended onto Mt Sinai; when he led the whole nation by a pillar of smoke during the day and a pillar of fire by night. He also fed them with manna from heaven, a type of bread appearing on the ground every morning, except on the Sabbath. Yet they still turned away from him and invented false gods.

Man has always been good at denying the existence of the One True God because it means accountability to someone, and in this sin-soaked world we would rather rule ourselves.

Another word for sin is lawlessness. This is total denial of God and his ways, in order to live our own lives completely independently, where there are no moral absolutes, no boundaries. It is no surprise society in general is in such a melt-down.

Believing what you cannot see is called faith and is a gift from God, who first deposits this seed-faith in us – just enough to believe when we are presented with the gospel or good news. What we do with that seed is up to us.

> For it is by grace you have been saved through faith – and this is not of yourselves, it is the gift of God... (Ephesians 2:8)

> ...we know that a person is made right with God by faith in Jesus Christ, not by obeying the law. And we have believed in Christ Jesus, so that we might be made right with God because of our faith in Christ, not because we have obeyed the law. For no one will ever be made right with God by obeying the law. (Galatians 2:16, NLT)

The gospel or good news is meant to be first confronting, then comforting.

We need to be confronted about the devastating consequences of sin which leads to death.

These consequences are all too obvious when we end up in prison. The comfort comes when we realise no matter what we have done, or haven't done, God still loves us unconditionally because he is our Heavenly Father and we are his children. He longs for us to return to his family and begin to live the abundant life he has for us.

It is not about who we are; it is about who he is. Criminal or success story, we are the same in his sight.

> And it is impossible to please God without faith. Anyone who wants to come to him must believe God exists and rewards those who sincerely seek him. (Hebrews 11:6, NLT)

Jesus came to earth about 2000 years ago. This is an historical fact, an undeniable truth. I find few people argue against this. The need to explain the relevance of his coming is fundamental to beginning what will become a life-long journey with him. He leads us to the Father and he says there is no other way. We can argue and compromise, but he is very clear that, without him, we don't get through the door. He is the door.

> Then Jesus said to them again, 'Most assuredly, I say to you, I am the door of the sheep. All who ever came before me are thieves and robbers, but the sheep did not hear them. I am the door. If anyone enters by me, he will be saved, and will go in and out and find pasture. 'I am the good shepherd. The good shepherd gives his life for the sheep.' (John 10:7-9)

Jesus says he is both the Shepherd and the door. To understand this you need to know how a shepherd looked after his sheep in the Middle East. The sheep were free to graze anywhere through the day under the watchful eye of the shepherd, who led them to fresh pastures and protected them from wild beasts. In the evening he led the sheep to an enclosure, built with either thorns or rocks and forming a circle with one opening.

Once the sheep were inside the enclosure, the shepherd sat in the doorway, protecting the sheep inside through the night. He was the door.

Jesus made this famous statement:

> I am the way, the truth, and the life. No one can come to the Father except through me. (John 14:6, NLT)

We can argue or live in denial, or even think there are many ways to God, but Jesus made it very clear he is the only way to our loving heavenly Father.

How do we respond to this? He is not going to change what he has said. He is not going to apologise for what seems like quite a narrow view.

If we are to live a satisfying and abundant life with him, we need to adjust our way of thinking to his way.

GETTING TO THE START LINE – ONLY JESUS

Ever since the rebellion in the garden when Adam and Eve, the first man and woman, disobeyed God and ate the only fruit in the garden they had been forbidden to eat, things have been different.

When God came looking for them, they hid from him because of their own fear, not because God was angry with them.

This is how many people view God today, through the eyes of fear. How much more do those who have ended up in prison, some having committed horrific crimes which continue to torment them day after day?

In the Garden of Eden, they tried to cover their nakedness and shame with fig leaves. This was man's attempt to cover his sin and somehow reconnect with his Maker.

Man continues to do the same thing today through religion. There are thousands of religions, each with their own particular flavour and views of how to get things sorted with God and somehow make it to 'paradise', or whatever name they have given to the after-life.

These religions are all about man's endeavours to curry favour with a big angry God who, if he is in a good mood, might allow their entry into his presence. This is religion. This is man's idea of what God wants.

This doesn't lead to freedom from sin but continued separation from God. 'Sin' literally means 'to miss the mark' or 'to be without the Word of God'.

Millions of people believe Jesus and religion are on the same page, if you talk about religion then you must mention Jesus. This could not be further from the truth. It was the religious leaders who demanded Jesus' crucifixion. It was the religious leaders Jesus publicly rebuked because of their unbelief and blindness. It was the religious leaders Jesus accused of leading people to hell and actively prevented people from entering the Kingdom of Heaven.

Religion is not the answer to man's rebellious ways and certainly not the path to righteousness or right standing with our Heavenly Father.

God's response to sin has been consistent through the ages. He says that the wages of sin (we earn it) is death (Romans 6:23). Back in the garden, when man sinned, death arrived... 'and in this way death came to all people because all sinned' (Romans 5:12).

What had been created to live forever became corrupted and now had an expiry date. Death also brought sickness, pain, suffering, striving, and many other negative consequences we consider normal today. God's response was to clothe Adam and Eve with animal skins to cover their nakedness. Two innocent animals had to die and their blood was shed to cover man's nakedness and rebellion to God.

There were approximately 4000 years between Adam and Jesus. Right through these years, called Old Testament times, God consistently required a sacrifice for sin in order for man to be made clean and to have fellowship with him. The word often used for this solution to separation between man and God was 'atonement'.

The Old Covenant, or Testament, required the shedding of innocent blood to 'cover the sins of the people'. This was never meant to be a permanent solution to the sin problem. Atonement is like covering dirty dishes with a clean dish cloth. It looks okay on the outside but lifting the cloth exposes the dirty dishes.

The New Covenant Jesus ratified is like putting the dirty dishes in the dishwasher and pushing the button. When the washing cycle is complete, the dishes are completely clean.

This is what Jesus did for us when he went to the cross. He carried our sins, he shed his perfect, sinless blood to wash our sins away and because he was perfect, he only had to do this once. God accepted this final sacrifice once and for all.

> For the death that he died, he died to sin once for all... (Romans 6:10)

> He is the kind of high priest we need because he is holy and blameless, unstained by sin. He has been set apart from sinners and has been given the highest place of honour in heaven. Unlike those other high priests, he does not need to offer sacrifices every day. They did this for their own sins first and then for the sins of the people. But Jesus did this once for all when he offered himself as the sacrifice for the people's sins. (Hebrews 7:26-27, NLT)

The Great Exchange took place, our sin for his righteousness. He paid the price we could not pay. He reconnected us to him, permanently. This is the difference between Christianity and all other religions. It is not what *we* have to do to get right with God; it is what *Jesus* has done to get us right with God. He was motivated by love for us, so all we have to do is accept what he has done on our behalf.

He has taken us from a lost eternity to a found eternity. This is the starting point of our journey with the Living God. We do not have to wait until we are perfect and clean before we can have fellowship with God. He has already made a way where we can be reconciled or accepted by God, not based on our works, but on his work completed at the cross.

I have heard a number of visiting overseas preachers say New Zealand is hard work. There seems to be a complacency or lethargy concerning the ways of God. This is probably true because some of our most used statements are 'She'll be right mate', or 'Sweet as bro'.

The kiwi mind-set is, 'Well, I'm not perfect, but I'm not really bad either' so if there is a God I should be okay with him when it comes time to meet him. God is an afterthought, a maybe, a possibility ... or not, and nobody knows for sure.

In prison there is a greater realisation something is seriously wrong because they have been told many times they are bad people by their families and the law, they deserve to be locked up and hopefully stay there so they can't be a menace to society any longer.

They are encouraged to participate in many courses, some better than others. Most of these courses fail to deal with the root problem – sin. Many are released more educated than when they were sentenced, but still end up reoffending and returning to do another lag.

Regular church attendance in New Zealand is about three to five percent of the general population. In prison voluntary church attendance is nearer 10 to 15 percent. Those attending are overjoyed to hear the gospel because it gives them hope for the future, hope something can change. I don't have to be this way forever. God really does care.

For those who do repent and turn to Jesus, Christian life in prison can be easier than when they are released because there are fewer distractions and temptations while they are inside.

Dr Edwin Cole, one of the world's most widely read Christian authors for men says it's easier to 'obtain' than it is to 'maintain' and this is true for many aspects of life.

One example of this was Puna. He was on his third and longest lag. I had known him at school and also played senior rugby against him. He was nearing the end of his sentence and had managed to get two of the most coveted jobs in the prison.

One was being on-call to play guitar when there was a service or welcoming dignitaries to the prison. He was a regular attender at church on Sunday and participated in a weekly men's course. He had a work-release job he would continue when he was released. He was busy, happy and passionate about living the Christian life.

When he was released he attended our church regularly at first. As time went by his attendance became sporadic. I started to hear stories of drugs and poor work ethic. We visited him at home many times in order to help and support him, but he chose to ignore us and continued on a destructive path.

Maintaining a Christian life in the world is a lot harder than in prison. Puna is not an isolated case. There are many men I had personal contact with who found it easy to obtain, but very difficult to maintain. Some are back inside again.

They are sorry to be there, but all have something in common – they failed to maintain fellowship with other believers. They left the family of God and tried to go it alone. This never works.

Getting to the start line and starting the race is a lot easier than completing the race. At the beginning, because Jesus has done everything for us, we only need to believe and receive what he has done. He cleans us out or washes all historical sin in our life, fills us with his Holy Spirit which empowers us to live for him.

The good race has now just begun, and it is not a 100-metre sprint, it is more like a triathlon or a marathon. The goal is not to compete with the other participants but to run the race God has for you.

This new life is all about God's love, our obedience and completion of the tasks he sets before us.

> Therefore we also, since we are surrounded by so great a cloud of witnesses, let us lay aside every weight, and the sin which so easily ensnares us, and let us run with endurance the race that is set before us... (Hebrews 12:1)

At the end of his life, the Apostle Paul wrote:

> For I am already being poured out as a drink offering, and the time of my departure is at hand. I have fought the good fight, I have finished the race, I have kept the faith. (2 Timothy 4:6-7)

REDEMPTION

What does that mean?

When you've spent a long time in Christian circles you tend to use language unbelievers have never heard. Many of the words we throw around are understood by our peers but not by those outside Christian circles. Jesus explained spiritual truth many times by using parables or stories the people could understand, yet the deeper, spiritual meaning was explained only to his closest disciples.

The words redeem (a verb) or redemption (a noun) are found throughout the Bible. It says Christians have been redeemed by the blood of the Lamb:

> And they sang a new song, saying:
> 'You are worthy to take the scroll,
> And to open its seals;
> For you were slain,
> And have redeemed us to God by your blood
> Out of every tribe and tongue and people and nation...'
> (Revelation 5:9)

One of my sons, when he was about seven years old, biked to the supermarket. While he was inside the store his bike was stolen. He had forgotten to lock it and had to walk home. Two years later he was biking down a street in Hastings and spotted his stolen bike in the front yard of a house with a 'for sale' sign on it.

He hurried home and told me he had spotted his stolen bike, and we jumped in my ute to get it back. When we arrived we checked out the bike and, sure enough, it was the stolen bike. The owner came out and I excitedly told him this was our bike and we wanted it back. He said we could have it for $40.

I told him he didn't understand; the bike was stolen. It was our bike and we wanted to take it home. He said I could take it anytime for $40.

We had a vigorous discussion for about five minutes. My son was there and I was not going home without the bike. The owner didn't budge so in the end, I peeled out $40 and got the bike back.

That bike was redeemed by me. Even though it was my bike and it had been stolen, I still had to pay to get it back.

This concept of redemption, or being 'bought back' by God, can be a life-changing revelation for prisoners because most have been told they are worthless. They come from dysfunctional backgrounds, and their future doesn't look good either.

They are already God's property; their birth wasn't an accident, and they have a Father in heaven who loves them. The devil, the thief, has stolen them and led them to places they should not go. He has stolen their freedom, robbed them, discouraged them and has control over them.

God has a plan to buy them back, not with money, but with blood, a life for a life, the precious life of his only Son.

Many people have a twisted or distorted view of God. They form their views based on Hollywood movies, what their mates think, or blame God for the latest tragedy in their lives.

God introduces himself to us through the Bible and through the Body of Christ, his representatives here on earth.

One of the greatest stories of how the Father reacts when we decide to return to him is found in Luke 15:

> Then he said: 'A certain man had two sons. And the younger of them said to his father, "Father, give me the portion of goods that falls to me." So he divided to them his livelihood. And not many days after, the younger son gathered all together, journeyed to a far country, and there wasted his possessions with prodigal living. But when he had spent all, there arose a severe famine in that land and he began to be in want. Then he went and joined himself to a citizen of that country, and he sent him into his fields to feed swine. And he would gladly have filled his stomach with the pods that the swine ate, and no one gave him anything.
>
> 'But when he came to himself, he said, "How many of my father's hired servants have bread enough and to spare, and I perish with hunger! I will arise and go to my father, and will say to him, 'Father, I have sinned against heaven and before you, and I am no longer worthy to be called your son. Make me like one of your hired servants.'"
>
> 'And he arose and came to his father. But when he was still a great way off, his father saw him and had compassion, and ran and fell on his neck and kissed him. And the son said to him, "Father, I have sinned against heaven and in your sight, and am no longer worthy to be called your son."
>
> 'But the father said to his servants, "Bring out the best robe and put it on him, and put a ring on his hand and sandals on his feet. And bring the fatted calf here and kill it, and let us eat and be merry; for this my son was dead and is alive again; he was lost and is found." And they began to be merry.' (Luke 15:11-24)

The youngest son (me) demanded and received his inheritance and set out for a distant land. His attitude was 'give me' and his departure to a distant land was so his father (God) could not see what he was doing.

While he had money, he also attracted a lot of friends who helped him spend it. When he ran out of money, his friends also left and he ended up feeding pigs which were better fed than him.

During his time in the pig pen he came to his senses. There was nothing wrong with his father's house where even the servants were well fed. He prepared an apology and started the long walk home.

Feeling sorry for himself was not enough to change his situation. He had to take action and start walking. His father had not followed him, but he was looking eagerly for his son's return, and when he spotted him he ran and embraced him. He did not even allow the son to finish his little speech about making himself a servant.

In his father's eyes he was always his son, no matter how far he strayed. The son's attitude had also changed from 'give me' to 'make me'. The father insisted they have a celebration and he fully restored this wayward son.

God the Father turned his back on Jesus as he hung on the cross so he would not have to turn his back on us. Jesus dying on the cross is the ultimate story of redemption. God paid the ultimate price – the torture and death of his only Son so we could be welcomed back into the family of God.

> For God so loved the world that he gave his only begotten so that whoever believes on him should not perish but have eternal life. (John 3:16)

As a father to seven children, every day is different. My children please me and upset me, but they are my children and I love them unconditionally. I am happiest when the whole family comes together for special occasions. We all sit around a giant table I made years ago and enjoy one another's company. It is immensely satisfying to see them prospering, starting new businesses, and now the grandchildren have started arriving.

This Bible story also shows us the Father does not change or adjust his ways to suit us. We need to adjust our thinking and return to our heavenly Father.

> Oh, give thanks to the Lord, for he is good.
> For his mercy endures forever.
> Let the redeemed of the Lord say so,
> Whom he has redeemed from the hand of the enemy.
> (Psalm 107:1-2)

Based on this Psalm, I give thanks to the Lord daily for my redemption. I shudder to think where I would be today if I hadn't returned to my Heavenly Father.

CHANGE YOUR HEART

The mind of man is fickle, changing as often as the weather; hot, cold, at peace, troubled, happy, sad, dictated by circumstances, every day a roller coaster.

The mind is a war zone, constantly in conflict, easily influenced by those closest to us. This is where the devil loves to play, and, if you don't know Jesus, he can drive you to despair and even suicide.

The Bible uses the word 'repentance' a lot and means 'to change your mind'. This first step into the Kingdom of God must be empowered by a continued 'changing or renewing of the mind'.

> And do not be conformed to this world, but be transformed by the renewing of your mind, that you may prove what is that good and acceptable and perfect will of God. (Romans 12:2)

This process of renewal will continue as long as we live. It requires us to change, not God. Only a heart change will enable us to stick with the programme because we will be challenged in all areas of our lives.

Let me illustrate: A ship manned by a captain and crew leaves port on a long journey. Only the captain has directions, information and purpose regarding the journey. Early in the trip the captain becomes seriously ill and is unable to communicate to the crew, so they take control of the ship and travel to various ports. They have a great time aimlessly cruising the world without knowing the direction or destination required. There is also danger at many of the ports. Sailors are injured and sometimes abused by the citizens of various countries. After a while the captain recovers enough to direct the ship again and attempts to get it back on course. But the crew, so used to running the ship, strongly object. They challenge the captain and there are constant conflicts and tensions, even though he alone knows the direction and purpose of the journey.

We are so used to running our own lives that when God is allowed to step in, we object because we know better. But only he can give our lives meaning, direction and purpose. He has an individual plan to fulfil the reason we were born; there are no accidents with God. He alone can fulfil our deepest longings and desires.

Many times I have heard prisoners say 'when I get out things are going to be different. I'm going to do the right thing by my family, no more drugs, I'm going to get a steady job'. These ideas are admirable, but sadly most do not follow through, or if they do it's only for a short period.

Changing your mind is only the beginning. These wonderful thoughts and aspirations need to move from the mind to the heart for there to be any possibility of sustained change.

> Surely he will never be shaken;
> The righteous will be in everlasting remembrance.
> He will not be afraid of evil tidings;
> His heart is steadfast, trusting in the Lord.
> His heart is established;
> He will not be afraid...
> (Psalm 112:6-8)

A heart change means you are truly sorry for all the negative, destructive things you have done, not feeling sorry because you were caught. A heart change is deeper, more permanent, means a lot more.

It will also lead us to sacrifice or give up those things that repeatedly drag us down. A heart change gives us more stick-ability, a greater ability to endure difficult times and helps us make good decisions and keep to the new plan.

We will not be so easily swayed by the words and actions of others, despite these things being hurtful and damaging, because we have a cause, a project, a lifelong pursuit of God enabling us to continue and complete our race in the face of anything the devil may throw at us.

There is a major problem in New Zealand. This land is filled with broken-hearted people.

A few years ago I was on one my frequent trips to India and was asked what the major difference was between the people in India and people in New Zealand.

I had noted there were far fewer prisons in India, fewer gangs, less societal dysfunction. Marriage is held in high regard, the divorce rate is close to zero, especially in the rural areas. This is changing in the big cities where there is much more Western influence.

In general terms, Indian children were growing up in a more stable home and community environment. Although life was incredibly tough at times with poverty around every corner, there still tended to be a more settled family environment which caused far fewer negative social issues.

New Zealand, on the other hand, is an affluent first-world country and, at first glance, seems to be blessed with an abundance of natural resources and relative peace.

You don't need to scratch far below the surface to reveal a

society in melt-down. The government is spending billions of dollars every year on social band-aids to try and cure a badly divided and dysfunctional society.

The most damning statistic shows children growing up without their natural fathers, producing generations of broken-hearted children.

Family First national director Bob McCoskrie said married parents were able to provide the best opportunities for children. 'We've tried to delude ourselves that family structure doesn't make a difference, but it does.'

Stable families are the building blocks of society, and by family I mean Dad and Mum, married, caring for each other and their children. When children are abandoned or abused by their parents, it breaks their hearts. No doctor, psychologist or medicine can heal this disease. Only Jesus can heal a broken heart. This was one of the reasons he was anointed by the Holy Spirit.

> 'The Spirit of the LORD is upon me,
> Because he has anointed me
> To preach the gospel to the poor;
> He has sent me to heal the broken-hearted,
> To proclaim liberty to the captives
> And recovery of sight to the blind,
> To set at liberty those who are oppressed;
> To proclaim the acceptable year of the Lord.'
> (Luke 4:18-19)

Medical experts may be able to help our physical or mental ailments, but they can't heal a broken heart. They can apply band-aids to the wound, but only the Great Physician is able to penetrate and restore the heart of man.

If a tree is diseased, pruning off the dead branches will not cure the tree. Only when the diseased root is cut and dug out will the tree survive.

Henry and Hope had been married 40 years. Now, well into retirement, the children had moved on and they were 'empty nesters'. They were regular church attendees and, on the outside, looked to be happy and content.

Their marriage was not so healthy. They were effectively living separate lives. Henry now spent most of his time in the refurbished shed, watching his favourite programmes, and even sleeping out there because it was more peaceful.

Hope was still living life at pace, filling it with trips away, attending family weddings and tangi. Constantly criticizing her husband and blaming him for most of their woes, she had effectively driven him out.

Hope had children from a previous relationship. Henry, in his younger days, had seriously abused these step-children and Hope was still blaming him for the hurt and family dysfunction.

Most of the serious violence done to children is by step-fathers, stepmothers or trusted extended family members. Broken marriages produce damaged children, both physically and mentally. Couples living together break up even more than married couples, leading to a toxic environment for children.

Because people have become so self-centred, the bond found in covenant relationship is rare. Most people do not even know what covenant means anymore.

A covenant is the strongest agreement between two parties dedicated to the betterment or improvement of the other. It is not about how I can benefit *from* you, it is about how I can help and strengthen you.

This is how God connects to us, through covenant, a blood

covenant, the strongest type. He sets the rules and when we come into agreement with these rules, we benefit from a divine connection to our Maker.

Marriage is supposed to be a blood covenant between man and woman to last through the years of challenge and difficulty and raising children, which is not easy.

Hope was still carrying the pain of what her husband had done years ago. He had asked her to forgive him, but she couldn't. I counselled her to 'let it go' but she said it was too hard even though it was destroying their marriage.

I told her she was unable to forgive because she had a broken heart. She stared at me for a minute, stunned, and the tears came. I asked if I could pray for her and she agreed. I prayed Jesus would heal her broken heart, and he did.

During the next few weeks, Henry was invited back into the house and back into the bedroom, and he wanted to. Hope said their marriage has never been stronger and their love and care for each other has blossomed again. This was a turning point in their long marriage.

Only Jesus can heal a broken heart.

VISIT THE PRISONERS

Bringing the word of God effectively to prisoners on a regular basis is definitely a calling.

This is not an easy environment to work in because you always seem to be the ambulance at the bottom of the cliff.

You don't need to have a prison record yourself to be relevant. Until his arrest and subsequent detention and torture, neither had Jesus, but he was intensely relevant to those who were disadvantaged and needed lifting up.

I have never been convicted of crime bad enough to go to prison, got close a number of times, but managed to avoid a prison sentence. There are a number of men I know who have been incarcerated in the past and are now ministering on a regular basis. They get a natural respect from the men because they can relate to prison life.

There is a currency which crosses boundaries and breaks down barriers. It's called empathy and compassion. This is felt more than spoken. You should have a genuine sense of 'I want to help you'. Sadly, I have seen some in prison ministry out of religious duty.

> I was naked and you clothed me; I was sick and you visited me;
> I was in prison and you came to me. (Matthew 25:36)

Prison Break

The prisoners quickly identify those who visit to preach at them.

There have been times I've entered a unit and heard inmates asking the officers who was coming in this week, and based on the answer decide whether to attend or not.

One well-meaning Christian told me his group had a wonderful church service, but I heard later from the inmates who attended it was terrible, they had to sit and be quiet and do exactly as directed.

The Christians were having a wonderful time, 'having church', but it all was quite irrelevant to the inmates.

At other times I have watched the inmates shuffling their feet and looking out the window where there is nothing to see, wishing they could leave.

There is another not so well-known verse:

> Remember the prisoners as if chained with them – those who are mistreated... (Hebrews 13:3)

This is empathy. This is sitting where they sit. These men are missing their families, especially if they are in for a long period. Some have had their partners give up and leave them, some for good reason. There are always things going on back home, good and bad, which they can do very little about.

You can't run a family from a phone in prison. Their children are often out of control because Dad is not there. They think they have failed and are distraught because they seem to be repeating what their fathers did to them.

There are times when I have been ministering and the power of God is evident. There are tears, laughter, genuine questions. You can see in their faces they are engaged, absorbed, wanting more. There have been times when the officers have come to take them back to their cells and they haven't wanted to go, asking for a few more minutes.

I will prepare something before I go in, but won't use it unless I feel it's relevant to what the men want to discuss. I always start by asking *them* questions, finding out what is current with them, getting them to open up a little, using their response as a springboard for the session.

You seldom need to get specific about sin. They already know and have been told numerous times they are bad. Any focus on sin should be around the fact sin is killing them, destroying their lives and hurting those closest to them. Many of them are trapped like the 'Romans 7 man':

> And I know that nothing good lives in me, that is, in my sinful nature I want to do what is right, but I can't. I want to do what is good, but I don't. I don't want to do what is wrong, but I do it anyway. But if I do what I don't want to do, I am not really the one doing wrong; it is sin living in me that does it.
>
> I have discovered this principle of life – that when I want to do what is right, I inevitably do what is wrong. I love God's law with all my heart. But there is another power within me that is at war with my mind. This power makes me a slave to the sin that is still within me. Oh, what a miserable person I am! Who will free me from this life that is dominated by sin and death? (Romans 7:18-24, NLT)

The answer to this universal condition called the sinful nature is found in Romans 8:

> So now there is no condemnation for those who belong to Christ Jesus. And because you belong to him, the power of

the life-giving Spirit has freed you from the power of sin that leads to death. The law of Moses was unable to save us because of the weakness of our sinful nature. So God did what the law could not do. He sent his own Son in a body like the bodies we sinners have. And in that body God declared an end to sin's control over us by giving his Son as a sacrifice for our sins. He did this so that the just requirement of the law would be fully satisfied for us, who no longer follow our sinful nature but instead follow the Spirit.

Those who are dominated by the sinful nature think about sinful things, but those who are controlled by the Holy Spirit think about things that please the Spirit. So letting your sinful nature control your mind leads to death. But letting the Spirit control your mind leads to life and peace. For the sinful nature is always hostile to God. It never did obey God's laws, and it never will. That's why those who are still under the control of their sinful nature can never please God.

But you are not controlled by your sinful nature. You are controlled by the Spirit if you have the Spirit of God living in you. (Romans 8:1-9, NLT)

Telling them they need to change, stop lying and deceiving, stop the violence, stop the revenge, is a complete waste of time. They already know what they are doing. They don't know how to change.

The only way to begin that journey is to be converted to faith in Jesus who, by the power of the Holy Spirit coming in and residing in them, will help them change, little by little, step by step.

Matthew 9 and Luke 19 should be the basis by which we minister in prison:

> As Jesus was walking along, he saw a man named Matthew sitting at his tax collector's booth. 'Follow me and be my disciple,' Jesus said to him. So Matthew got up and followed him.
>
> Later, Matthew invited Jesus and his disciples to his home as dinner guests, along with many tax collectors and other disreputable sinners. But when the Pharisees saw this, they asked his disciples, 'Why does your teacher eat with such scum?'
>
> When Jesus heard this, he said, 'Healthy people don't need a doctor – sick people do.' Then he added, 'Now go and learn the meaning of this Scripture: "I want you to show mercy, not offer sacrifices." For I have come to call not those who think they are righteous, but those who know they are sinners.'
> (Matthew 9:9-13, NLT)

Tax collectors were native Israelites hated by all but their own; they were outcasts of society. Not only did they work for the brutal occupying Roman power, they regularly overcharged the tax required and kept the profits for themselves.

Matthew was called by Jesus and immediately left his job and followed Jesus; he ended up writing the book of Matthew. The only ones who had a problem with Jesus hanging out with 'scum' were the religious leaders.

> Jesus entered Jericho and made his way through the town. There was a man there named Zacchaeus. He was the chief tax collector in the region, and he had become very rich. He tried to get a look at Jesus, but he was too short to see over the crowd. So he ran ahead and climbed a sycamore-fig tree beside the road, for Jesus was going to pass that way.
>
> When Jesus came by, he looked up at Zacchaeus and called him by name. 'Zacchaeus!' he said. 'Quick, come down! I must be a guest in your home today.'

Prison Break

> Zacchaeus quickly climbed down and took Jesus to his house in great excitement and joy. But the people were displeased. 'He has gone to be the guest of a notorious sinner,' they grumbled.
>
> Meanwhile, Zacchaeus stood before the Lord and said, 'I will give half my wealth to the poor, Lord, and if I have cheated people on their taxes, I will give them back four times as much!'
>
> Jesus responded, 'Salvation has come to this home today, for this man has shown himself to be a true son of Abraham. For the Son of Man came to seek and save those who are lost.'
> (Luke 19:1-10, NLT)

This is an incredible story of Jesus calling another 'notorious sinner', a chief tax collector called Zacchaeus. Jesus did not point out any of his many sins, he merely invited himself to his home.

This time it wasn't the religious leaders who were upset; it was the general population.

Zachaeus response was amazing. Because Jesus noticed him, he became generous to the poor and promised repayment at 400 percent of anyone he had ripped off. Jesus announced salvation had come to his home

There are a few times I have been ministering in the prison where those attending knew almost nothing about Jesus, but within an hour have come to salvation.

It was obvious the Holy Spirit was moving and these men merely responded to his promptings.

FORGIVENESS

Many times I have been asked about 'an eye for an eye and tooth for a tooth' and asked to confirm it's in the Bible.

It is, but like any story, you have to apply context to the statement.

This law was set in the Old Testament or old covenant times. We don't live in those times. We live in New Covenant times Jesus introduced by word and action.

Forgiveness is the glue in the Kingdom of God; it brings people together. It is also the basis on which God deals with us when we confess our sins.

> If we confess our sins, he is faithful and just to forgive us our sins and to cleanse us from all unrighteousness. (1 John 1:9)

Sadly there are many people in prison today because of unforgiveness. Thoughts of revenge or 'utu' run deep with many. Some spend a lot of time thinking and planning how they are going to 'waste' the person doing them wrong as soon as they get released. They don't sleep well and sometimes get so worked up they lash out at those around them.

Another interesting aspect of unforgiveness is it affects us more than the other person. It's like drinking poison and expecting the other person to die.

Prison Break

Two men had a big fallout. One lived out of town; the other lived close to town. There were two routes into town and the one who lived further away always took the long route into town because he did not want to drive past the other's home. This action did not affect the one closer to town; he was not even aware it was happening.

The other man was spending a lot more on petrol to travel to and from town. That's what unforgiveness does. It costs us more when we don't forgive the other.

God expects us to forgive from our hearts those who have wronged us. This is not allowing them to get away with what they have done, but it releases you from bitterness and resentment.

There is a parable found in Matthew 18 which explains this:

> Then Peter came to him and asked, 'Lord, how often should I forgive someone who sins against me? Seven times?'
>
> 'No, not seven times,' Jesus replied, 'but seventy times seven.'
>
> 'Therefore, the Kingdom of Heaven can be compared to a king who decided to bring his accounts up to date with servants who had borrowed money from him. In the process, one of his debtors was brought in who owed him millions of dollars. He couldn't pay, so his master ordered that he be sold – along with his wife, his children, and everything he owned – to pay the debt.
>
> 'But the man fell down before his master and begged him, "Please, be patient with me, and I will pay it all." Then his master was filled with pity for him, and he released him and forgave his debt.
>
> 'But when the man left the king, he went to a fellow servant who owed him a few thousand dollars. He grabbed him by the throat and demanded instant payment.

'His fellow servant fell down before him and begged for a little more time. "Be patient with me, and I will pay it," he pleaded. But his creditor wouldn't wait. He had the man arrested and put in prison until the debt could be paid in full.

'When some of the other servants saw this, they were very upset. They went to the king and told him everything that had happened. Then the king called in the man he had forgiven and said, "You evil servant! I forgave you that tremendous debt because you pleaded with me. Shouldn't you have mercy on your fellow servant, just as I had mercy on you?" Then the angry king sent the man to prison to be tortured until he had paid his entire debt.

'That's what my heavenly Father will do to you if you refuse to forgive your brothers and sisters from your heart.' (Matthew 18:21-35, NLT)

God forgives us for all our sins when we ask him. This is a debt which is impossible for us to pay, but God is moved by compassion for us and freely forgives. When we continue to hold a grudge against someone who has sinned against us, we end up in prison in the hands of the torturers. The one we do not forgive also ends up in prison, so the outcome for both is bad.

It is difficult to forgive from your heart unless you have first tasted God's forgiveness. He empowers you to forgive.

There is another Bible principle called retain or release. When someone sins against us and we hold on to it in unforgiveness, we retain or hold on to their sins.

An example is what a father may have done to his children. He may have abused them, or maybe he was absent, or neglected them. The children end up doing the same thing to their children and the cycle continues.

Here it is in John 20:

> And when he had said this, he breathed on them, and said to them, 'Receive the Holy Spirit. If you forgive the sins of any, they are forgiven them; if you retain the sins of any, they are retained.' (John 20:22-23)

When you receive the Holy Spirit into your life, Jesus gives you power and permission to either retain or release. The sins you forgive are released, the sins you do not forgive are retained in your life.

Many times I have seen men set free. Sadly, most of these bondages come from their fathers. This shows why it is so important for dads to be empowered by God to be the best fathers to their children, to be the best husband to their wives and to be prophet and priest to their families

Aso was an angry man. He didn't smile much, didn't say much. When you were around him you needed to be careful about what you said or he would blow up. He often resorted to alcohol to numb the pain. This anger had led to a couple of stays in prison.

He worked for us and was a reliable, steady worker. One day, he had a dispute with my brother, who was in charge of the team, and ended up punching and knocking him to the ground. This was grounds for instant dismissal and my brother and I had a few difficult discussions over the following days.

Immediately after the incident my brother offered him a ride home. This completely stunned Aso, but he calmed down and accepted the offer. He was sorry for what happened, but was still trapped deep inside. He could not get rid of this anger.

We invited him to church. He came, reluctantly at first, but soon started to make connections and enjoy the fellowship of believers. He wanted to make a decision to follow Jesus but the anger issue needed to be dealt with first, so three of us met and discussed it.

It turned out he had a secret he had shared with nobody. When he was young, he was sexually abused by an uncle many times. This was the main reason he left the islands and came to live in New Zealand. He hated this man so intensely and rightfully so. This person had abused an innocent child and had not been brought to justice.

Although Aso had travelled a long way from the crime scene, he still carried this burden he was never meant to carry. We were the first ones he had told. We counselled him to forgive his uncle, just as Jesus had forgiven him.

This was really difficult for Aso and we gave him time to consider. He consented and we prayed, breaking those chains binding him. We also prayed for Jesus to heal his broken heart. He wept and allowed Jesus to pour his healing balm right into his wounded and broken heart.

For the first time in many years, Aso smiled. Not just a quick superficial grin, but real joy welling up from deep within, from his heart; a changed man.

DECEPTION

In Matthew 24, Jesus' disciples asked him questions about what would be happening in the Last Days.

His reply was interesting as he said four times deception would be rampant.

> And Jesus answered and said to them: 'Take heed that no one deceives you. (Matthew 24:4)
>
> For many will come in My name, saying, 'I am the Christ,' and will deceive many. (Matthew 24:5)
>
> Then many false prophets will rise up and deceive many. (Matthew 24:11)
>
> For false christs and false prophets will rise and show great signs and wonders to deceive, if possible, even the elect. (Matthew 24:24)

Deception is one the oldest and most effective tools the devil uses to separate people from God. When God confronted Adam and Eve in the garden, after they had eaten the forbidden fruit, Eve said 'the serpent deceived me...'

If people realised where their rebellion from God really

leads (pain and death), they may not even start on this destructive journey.

Deception is like the poisoned apple offered to Snow White. It looks great on the outside, but the poison on the inside is what will kill you. A glass of water may be quite okay, but add a drop of poison to it and it will kill you. Even though it's 99 percent okay, the one percent will kill you.

Another word for deception is counterfeit. Counterfeit money may look like the real thing, but it's worthless. It has to look like the original to fool people.

Here is a scale where 1 is a lie and 10 is the truth:

```
         1  2  3  4  5  6  7  8  9  10
Lie      |__|__|__|__|__|__|__|__|__|      Truth
```

Where do you think deception fits on this scale?

The answer is 9. So close to the truth, but not. Looks genuine, but not. Sounds okay, but leads to death.

There is huge deception today about who God is, how he works and how he relates to us. We believe the Hollywood movies which take some true information from the Bible and combine it with fictional nonsense. Many of the biblical stories have been twisted and changed and mostly give a completely false representation of God.

Truth is not just an idea or a fact, truth is a person, his name is Jesus.

> Jesus said to him, 'I am the way, the truth, and the life. No one comes to the Father except through me.' (John 14:6)

Jesus never lies to us, does not try to control us, does not put sickness on us and does not forcefully separate us from our families. These things are the domain of the devil. The devil is not your mate, he wants to kill you. Don't be fooled.

I have seen many prisoners have a twisted view of God and life in general, but I have also seen them start to think straight when regularly confronted with the word of truth, the Bible, and this seems to clear away the fog of deception. Religion says there are many paths to God and we have to behave and do good works in order to obtain God's favour. This is deception and, therefore, worthless. Jesus said this:

> Let them alone. They are blind leaders of the blind. And if the blind leads the blind, both will fall into a ditch... (Matthew 15:14)

Deception says, 'Eat, drink, be merry, do whatever makes you feel good, no limits, go hard.' Truth says you reap what you sow.

Truth says we deserve death, but the penalty was paid by Jesus' death on the cross. This is grace:

> For by grace you have been saved through faith and that not of yourselves; it is the gift of God... (Ephesians 2:8)

This also demonstrates Christ's love for us before we even knew him.

> But God demonstrates his own love toward us, in that while we were still sinners, Christ died for us. (Romans 5:8)

Deception says drugs are okay, they help you to cope with life. Truth says men were created to rule and have dominion on the earth. Drugs end up ruling you, controlling you. God never designed us to be ruled by any part of creation, only by God; it is our choice. Drugs take away choice.

Deception says it's okay to beat my wife, my kids and anybody else who gets in my way. Truth says we get authority through serving and loving others; then they want to follow, want to obey, because you are leading by example.

Deception says it's always somebody else's fault. Truth says take responsibility for your own issues. God will help you sort them out, but it starts with taking ownership and including him in the healing process.

Deception says God is dead and we accidentally arrived here by random mutation. Deception says in the beginning there was nothing, and then it exploded.

Truth says all we see, feel, touch, taste and smell was created by a loving Heavenly Father. This same Heavenly Father has a unique plan for each of us and everything we do and think is recorded for eternity

Deception says when we die that's it, or we sleep forever, or go to purgatory, or hang out with all our ancestors or automatically end up in heaven, even if we didn't acknowledge God all our lives.

Truth says there is a heaven and the door is open when we admit or confess our sins, ask Jesus to forgive us and enter into a lifelong relationship with our Heavenly Father.

Truth says there is also a hell and there is no escape, no remand, no release, no probation, no 'Oh I'll change my mind'. Hell is torment and torture forever.

CHANGE

Change is not change until it is change.

If I could have a dollar for every time someone has said to me 'I'm going to change' I would be a wealthy man.

Good intentions are just that... intentions. Meaningful change takes courage, time, perseverance. Pride usually has to be kicked to touch, replaced by humility and a willingness to listen.

Deep down people know change would be for the best, but the cost is too high, or they can't be bothered doing the hard yards and they are simply too lazy to really make the shift. This generation has been described as 'fence sitters', not willing to jump one way or the other. Jesus describes this in Revelation 3:

> So then, because you are lukewarm, and neither cold nor hot,
> I will vomit you out of My mouth. (Revelation 3:16)

Challenge leads to pressure, pressure leads to change, no pressure, no change. When the gospel is presented to anyone, it should be balanced. First the bad news – we have all sinned, causing our relationship with God our Father to be severed. The good news is he has bridged the gap by paying for our sins with the sacrificial death of his Son. This is like electrifying the fence causing us to make a decision one way or the other.

> I know your works, that you are neither cold nor hot. I could wish you were cold or hot. (Revelation 3:15)

Remember the story of the lost son in Luke 15. He wanted change at the start by demanding his entire share in the estate, leaving his family, moving to a distant land, but ending up feeding pigs.

In order for him to recover completely, he had to change again. Thinking about change and really changing are two different things. Nothing was going to change until he started walking back to his father.

This is the case today. If you have ended up in prison, upon release you may need to move away from those who negatively influence you.

I received a call from an inmate recently I ministered to over ten years ago. At the time he wanted to carry on living where he was arrested. My advice was he needed to move and start a new life, a difficult decision because most of his family was based here. He ended up moving 600 kilometres north and started a new life. He is now reconciled with his wife, but not his children.

Sometimes things do not completely return to 'normal' because of the severity of the crime, but you can change enough to not return to prison.

Another man who has worked for me moved away from a negative family environment in Northland and has now settled in our area. Upon release he knew nobody here and had to start from scratch, but he too is not going back inside.

Difficult decisions, but right decisions, lead to permanent change. Both these men found a good caring church that assisted them to get re-established. They found strength in the brotherhood of believers and are now helping others get their broken lives back on track.

Lasting change doesn't happen overnight. The initial big change to relocate comes with its own challenges and pressures. Not every day is going to be a good day.

The devil has his workers located in every city on this planet. They are easily accessible if you choose to go that way. There will be many bumps in the road, but if you stick with the right plan you will be able to look back and see how far you've come. Don't give up, don't quit, keep moving.

Joshua was the man God tasked with establishing a whole nation in a new land. God had brought the Israelite nation out of Egypt, out of slavery. It took God four days to get Israel out of Egypt. It took him 40 years to get Egypt out of Israel.

God had some advice he gave Joshua seven times: 'be strong and courageous'.

> This Book of the Law shall not depart from your mouth, but you shall meditate in it day and night, that you may observe to do according to all that is written in it. For then you will make your way prosperous, and then you will have good success. Have I not commanded you? Be strong and of good courage; do not be afraid, nor be dismayed, for the Lord your God is with you wherever you go.' (Joshua 1:8-9)

Courage means acting on a need greater than self. Courage is needed to bring about personal change, and you also need to understand nobody lives life in a vacuum. There are others close to us who will benefit from positive change but for us to move them in a positive direction means our life has to be consistent. Day by day living and doing the right thing.

I first met Steve, a big Samoan man, thirty years ago. He had just been released from prison having served a term for grievous bodily harm (GBH). He was a violent man often fuelled by alcohol, so violent three of his five children were living with relatives scattered around the country. When he was released he made a decision to move away from relatives who continually led him astray (first courageous decision). He brought his wife and two children up to Hastings where he knew no one.

Steve approached me for work and started at the bottom. Over a period of five years he softened towards the Lord, although there was no way he would ever come to a 'Palangi church'.

One day his wife lost her wallet, and it was picked up by my pastor on the footpath next to our church. He returned it to them and invited them to come to church on Sunday.

Steve reluctantly showed up on Sunday and found to his amazement he liked our church. Soon after, he surrendered his life to Jesus (second courageous decision).

Within a month all his children returned to him and he gave me the privilege of leading them all to Jesus.

They were living in a small three-bedroom house in Flaxmere for many years. Recently they were able to buy a beautiful home next to the church. Their children are all growing up as well balanced, successful young people making a positive contribution to society.

Steve is proof God does have a good plan for us all. We simply need to join the family of God and follow his instructions. He empowers us to live righteously and happily for him and for others.

NOT ALONE – FATHERS

I don't want to rank the chapters in this book in order of importance, but this chapter would have to be right up there.

Let's start with some statistics:

- 63% of youth suicides are from fatherless homes (US Dept. of Health/Census) – five times the average.
- 90% of all homeless and runaway children are from fatherless homes – 32 times the average.
- 85% of all children who show behaviour disorders come from fatherless homes – 20 times the average. (Center for Disease Control)
- 80% of rapists with anger problems come from fatherless homes – 14 times the average. (Justice & Behavior, Vol 14, p.403-26)
- 71% of all high school dropouts come from fatherless homes – nine times the average. (National Principals Association Report)
- 75% of all adolescent patients in chemical abuse centres come from fatherless homes – ten times the average. (Rainbows for all God's Children)
- 70% of youths in state-operated institutions come from fatherless homes – nine times the average. (US Dept. of Justice, Sept. 1988)

Prison Break

- 85% of all youths in prison come from fatherless homes – 20 times the average. (Fulton Co. Georgia, Texas Dept. of Correction)
- Fatherless boys and girls are twice as likely to drop out of high school; twice as likely to end up in jail; four times more likely to need help for emotional or behavioural problems. (US D.H.H.S. news release, March 26, 1999)

These are damning statistics. For every man in prison, there are many more wives and children left at home husbandless and fatherless.

You cannot run a family on the end of a phone. I see the frustration every time I go into prison. Many of the men in prison have lived most of their lives without their biological father and though they don't want to, they are doing the same thing to their children. Fathers are some of the most maligned people in modern society; there is a societal bias against fathers.

Here are a couple of quotes written by secular commentators:

> On the way to work in the car this morning, I heard the radio host say mums were twice as important as dads. What? Seems a little sexist. Can you imagine a man saying men are twice as important or valuable in say, the workplace?
>
> This type of comment is exactly what is wrong in America, the world, and the court system as well. Dads are *just* as important as mums. No wonder fatherless children statistics are the way they are. We need more child custody attorneys to make a difference.

Statistics and social evidence overwhelmingly prove it is detrimental for children to grow up without a father in the home. Pay close attention to how many times in TV commercials, sitcoms, and movies men and their role in society are degraded. Men should be treated as fairly and *equally*, especially in a court of law.

In my opinion, there is an all-out war against men in general and it's time to stand up and fight for our families and fight for our children.

Foolish government decisions have continued to undermine the value of fathers. The family has been redefined as some mish-mash homogenous mess which may or may not have the father or mother involved in rearing the children. Rather than pointing out all the wrong definitions I will show what God considers a family: one man, one woman, married, lovingly rearing their biological children, and there is room for adoption. This marital union is supposed to be for life. God calls this a covenant and it started in the Garden of Eden.

The Bible starts with a marriage and ends in a marriage:

And the LORD God caused a deep sleep to fall on Adam, and he slept; and he took one of his ribs, and closed up the flesh in its place. Then the rib which the LORD God had taken from man he made into a woman, and he brought her to the man. And Adam said:

'This is now bone of my bones
And flesh of my flesh;
She shall be called Woman,
Because she was taken out of Man.'

Therefore a man shall leave his father and mother and be joined to his wife, and they shall become one flesh. (Genesis 2:21-24)

> 'Let us be glad and rejoice and give him glory, for the marriage of the Lamb has come, and his wife has made herself ready.' And to her it was granted to be arrayed in fine linen, clean and bright, for the fine linen is the righteous acts of the saints. Then he said to me, 'Write: "Blessed are those who are called to the marriage supper of the Lamb!"' (Revelation 19:7-9)

Marriage has been the stable building block of society for thousands of years. Strong marriages, strong society; broken marriages, broken society.

There are many 'cures' being promoted by secular 'experts' regarding the breakdown of society. Billions of dollars annually are now being thrown at the collapsing mess. Families are disintegrating, prison rates are climbing.

Paul writing to the Romans puts it like this:

> ...because, although they knew God, they did not glorify him as God, nor were thankful, but became futile in their thoughts, and their foolish hearts were darkened. Professing to be wise, they became fools... (Romans 1:21-22)

The highest revelation we can receive about God is that he is our Father.

The devil hates God and puts a lot of resources into putting down anything God deems to have value. Fathers have value, wives have value, children have value, but for things to function properly there has to be order, the right order:

> Wives, submit to your own husbands, as to the Lord. For the husband is head of the wife, as also Christ is head of the church; and he is the Saviour of the body. Therefore, just as

the church is subject to Christ, so let the wives be to their own husbands in everything.

Husbands, love your wives, just as Christ also loved the church and gave himself for her... (Ephesians 5:22-25)

There it is... wives submit, husbands love. Sadly the bit about 'submitting' has sometimes been used by men to justify physical violence against their wives or partners, landing many in prison for repeated attacks and dangerous drunken outbursts. The true meaning of the verse is clearer in the *Message* translation:

> Wives, understand and support your husbands in ways that show your support for Christ. The husband provides leadership to his wife the way Christ does to his church, not by domineering but by cherishing. So just as the church submits to Christ as he exercises such leadership, wives should likewise submit to their husbands.

You can't demand that someone submit – you can only do your part and love. This love is the sacrificial love Jesus demonstrated when he died on the cross – he put others ahead of himself. Fathers demonstrate this love by protecting, providing, guiding, and leading those entrusted to their care.

The Bible states very clearly in the Last Days men will be lovers of themselves, disobedient to parents.

> You should know this, Timothy that in the last days there will be very difficult times. For people will love only themselves and their money. They will be boastful and proud, scoffing at God, disobedient to their parents, and ungrateful. They will consider nothing sacred. They will be unloving and unforgiving;

they will slander others and have no self-control. They will be cruel and hate what is good. They will betray their friends, be reckless, be puffed up with pride, and love pleasure rather than God. They will act religious, but they will reject the power that could make them godly. (2 Timothy 3:1-5, NLT)

Being a father and being selfish does not lead to a successful family. However, God does have a plan for these days:

Look, I am sending you the prophet Elijah before the great and dreadful day of the Lord arrives. His preaching will turn the hearts of fathers to their children, and the hearts of children to their fathers. (Malachi 4:5-6, NLT)

God the Father has already turned his heart toward us which enables us to turn toward him, and on this earthly plane he has established this divine order, fathers turn toward their children, then the children to their fathers.

Many men in prison already have broken relationships with their children and see little hope for restoration, but this is mainly because it has not been in their heart to maintain a healthy relationship with their children. They have been trapped in their own dysfunctional world, caring mainly for themselves.

These men have already been victims of their own wayward fathers so have not had these vital skills in maintaining a healthy family passed on to them.

Twenty years ago, a Christian group visiting a prison regularly decided to help prisoners celebrate Mother's Day. They bought Mothers' Day cards and handed them out to a few prisoners encouraging them to send the cards to their mums. The response was overwhelming and they had to print many more cards to satisfy the demand.

When Father's Day arrived they did the same thing, printed the cards and handed them out. The demand for the cards was almost nil. There was a great chasm between the generations, but this simple example shows quite clearly the root problem with most of our prison population – disconnection with our fathers.

There is also the view 'when I get out, I'm going to find as many women as I can to satisfy my needs. Why would I want to turn to God who is going to limit me to one woman?'

The answer is simple. God is not trying to take away the fun and enjoyment, he invented sex and, in the context of marriage, over a period of years married men have more sex, not less, than those who are not.

God shows this in Proverbs 5:

> Drink water from your own cistern,
> And running water from your own well.
> Should your fountains be dispersed abroad,
> Streams of water in the streets?
> Let them be only your own,
> And not for strangers with you.
> Let your fountain be blessed,
> And rejoice with the wife of your youth.
> As a loving deer and a graceful doe,
> Let her breasts satisfy you at all times;
> And always be enraptured with her love.
> (Proverbs 5:15-19)

Intimacy with anyone should not take place until you are first prepared to put a ring on her finger and enter into covenant with her. This means vowing to care for and love her and only her, above all others.

This is the foundation of a successful marriage. No wonder so many fail today because of ignorance and selfishness. God's order is first become a good husband before you have to step up and take more responsibility as a father.

Dysfunctional parents do not produce healthy well-balanced children. But over the years I have seen many families restored to loving healthy relationships and, even when it does not work out with the children, grandchildren can benefit from older, wiser grandparents. God the Father is always at work restoring, rebuilding, and reuniting that which was broken.

A teacher will give you what he knows, a father will give you who he is. From a friend you will get good advice, but from a father you will get his heart.

STEPS TO TRUE FREEDOM

- Surrender your life to Jesus. Give up trying to do your own thing.

- Be filled with the Holy Spirit. His power in you will change your life and help you to overcome those negative forces in your life.

- Pray regularly, not some repetitive religious prayer, but genuine heartfelt conversation with your Father. This should be two-way; you also need to listen.

- Read the Bible or listen to good solid biblical teaching. Begin in the New Testament, Matthew, Mark, Luke, or John.

- Find other like-minded Christian people to share your journey. We were never designed to walk alone.

- When you are released you may need to move away from family and so-called friends who get you into trouble.

- You must also establish new Godly relationships. Search for a church that loves and accepts you. If you find the first church you enter is not right for you, find another. Keep looking until you find one where you can settle.

- Find a father – a mature Christian man with a solid track record who you give permission to speak into your life. Someone who will pull you away from negative circumstances and hold you accountable and encourage you and, most of all, love you as a father should – unconditionally.

- Maintain fellowship; you are now part of a new family. This family may not be perfect, but neither are you.

- Enjoy the journey. There will be challenges and not everything will go well, but keep going, don't give up, never quit.

Salvation Prayer

Lord Jesus, I come to you now. I have done many stupid things that have hurt myself and others. Most of all I have been living my life without you. But now, instead of walking away from you, I turn and walk towards you. Please forgive me for all the sins I have committed, fill me with your Holy Spirit, empower me to walk with you from now on. Thank you for being my Saviour and washing all my sin away with your blood. Jesus, I also make you Lord of my life. You are the boss, my boss. Help me to walk in obedience to you until you come and take me home to heaven. Amen.

TO THOSE INVOLVED IN CHRISTIAN PRISON MINISTRY

- Pray, pray, pray.

  The earnest prayer of a righteous person has great power and produces wonderful results. (James 5:16, NLT)

- Prepare, but be ready to be led by the Holy Spirit. Many times I have prayerfully prepared my sermons only to find God wants to move in another direction.

- Begin by asking questions relevant to the men. Find out where they are at.

- Engage in conversation. You are there for them, not for your own ego.

- Preach the gospel clearly and concisely if you have unbelievers in the room.

- Salvation must be a priority. We may only see them once, but we need to trust God has got things under control. He will place other Christians across their paths in their journey to freedom.

Prison Break

- Don't try to explain spiritual truths to unspiritual men. Use parables, stories and testimonies either of yourself or other changed lives.

- The spirit by which you minister will be obvious. Condemnation or compassion. We are not there to preach *at* them, but rather to lovingly bring conviction so they may accept the free gift of eternal life. This cannot happen without repentance.

- For those who are already saved, fresh bread, fresh manna from heaven needs to be delivered in order to encourage and build up. Jesus said: 'Feed my sheep.'

THE VISION

This was an open vision given to a young Maori man over 30 years ago while he was walking through Flaxmere Park in Hastings:

> I saw myself in a prison cell looking out through the bars down a long dimly lit corridor. I could see right down to the end of this long corridor a few stairs leading up to a throne. Seated on this throne was the devil. I realised this was a vision of hell itself.
>
> Jesus entered this hall right in front of me. He was bright like lightening and as he walked down the corridor, I could see thousands of demons on each side. The biggest and most powerful were at the front, they cowered at his presence
>
> As Jesus approached the throne the devil stood up and immediately fell face first on the ground at Jesus feet. Jesus reached down and stripped the devil of a set of keys hung around his waist. He then lifted his foot and stomped hard on the devil's head and turned and started to walk back toward me.
>
> As Jesus approached me I could see the demons falling on their faces like dominos as he walked past them. Jesus exited the hall just as he had entered it.
>
> It was then my prison door swung open and the vision ended.

I believe this is an accurate picture of what Jesus did between his death on the cross and his resurrection on Sunday morning. The devil held the keys of death and hell up to that point because of the authority passed to him by Adam when he rebelled against God's instruction and ate the forbidden fruit in the Garden of Eden.

Today the devil has no power over us except that which we give him. We cannot overcome him in our own strength, so he has many of us locked and imprisoned because of our sin. These prison cells represent anger, depression, rejection, addictions, hatred, suicidal thoughts, murders and anything contrary to the will of God in our lives. Only Jesus has the power to overcome the devil. He has given us believers' authority over all the wicked schemes of the devil.

> [Jesus] said to them, 'I saw Satan fall like lightning from heaven. Behold, I have given you authority over all the power of the enemy and nothing shall harm you.' (Luke 10:18,19)

> He himself likewise shared in the same, that through death he might destroy him who had the power of death, that is, the devil... (Hebrews 2:14)

It is only when we allow Jesus to become an intimate part of our lives do the prison doors swing open, leading us to true freedom both inside and around us.

This is the message of the eternal gospel we his servants are entrusted with.

Nobody else has this message of hope, nobody else has this redeeming power. Let us take this word confidently to those who need it most.

The Vision

So his master said, 'Go out into the country lanes and behind the hedges and urge anyone you find to come so the house will be full. (Luke 14:23, NLT)

ABOUT THE AUTHOR

 Roger Curtis was born in Hawke's Bay, New Zealand, and has lived there all his life. Involved in the church since a radical encounter with the Lord in 1980, he serves as an elder and is active in Prison Ministry.

He and his wife Rachel run a horticultural contracting business, which has often been used as an employment pathway for inmates on 'work to release', or for people who are simply looking for a fresh start.

In 2004 Roger and Rachel built a large 13-bedroom home to accommodate their growing family and provide a place to stay for those in the local community struggling to break out of destructive lifestyles.

Roger and Rachel have eight children, three now married and all participating in the life of the church.

www.ingramcontent.com/pod-product-compliance
Lightning Source LLC
Chambersburg PA
CBHW071409290426
44108CB00014B/1753